How to Double Your Placements in 121 Days or Less

Michael Gionta

Double Your Placements
141031-002

Published by:
90-Minute Books
Newinformation Inc
302 Martinique Drive
Winter Haven, FL 33884
www.90minutebooks.com

Copyright © 2015, Michael Gionta

Published in the United States of America

ISBN-13: 978-1508516859
ISBN-10: 1508516855

No parts of this publication may be reproduced without correct attribution to the author and the domain www.DoubleYourPlacements.com.

For more information on 90-Minute Books including finding out how you can publish your own lead generating book, visit www.90minutebook.com or call (863) 318-0464.

Here's What's Inside...

Principle #1: Moving from Overwhelm to Clarity.... 6

Principle #2: Moving from Roller Coaster Revenue to Predictable Income... 13

Principle #3: Moving from Transactional Vendor to Trusted Advisor... 21

Implementation...
Putting the Principles in Place... 29

Here's How the Double Your Revenue in 121 Days or Less Program Works... 35

Here's the Most Common Questions Recruiters Have About Our Coaching Program.................... 43

Testimonials 52

Recruiter Resources.. 55

Here's How to Double Your Revenue In the Next 121 Days Or Less... 57

Introduction

Double Your Placements!

East Haddam, CT
February 2015

I have been blessed to help both independent recruiters as well as recruiting firm owners see dramatic increases in revenue, profitability and maybe most importantly, quality of life since I started coaching in 2007. So many of you have incredibly strong work ethics and are truly committed to your clients, yet struggle to bring in consistent revenue and get repeat business. Honestly, much of this is not your fault. Most of us were taught a highly commoditized approach to the market that leaves us all sounding mostly the same. When many of us 'sound the same' we end up getting treated 'the same'. Often this results in a transactional/vendor relationship where our sole point value (in the prospect's mind) is the quality of the 'resumes' they see versus the quality of the talent we discover along with the quality of service we deliver.

In the years I have coached recruiters, I see them and recruiting for owners make the recruiting business much harder than they have to. They often end up very quickly in overwhelm mode chasing clients. Most have never been taught how to be seen as a trusted advisor to their clients. I wasn't either! I invested tens of thousands of dollars in professional training and years of my life using 'trial and error' in perfecting this approach resulting in several years of personal production in excess of $1,000,000 and my best year over $2,143,000. This process led me to develop several clients with over $250,000 in annual placement revenue and over $2,000,000 in lifetime revenue. This is the reason I wanted to write this book. I wanted to help recruiters make the shift to a trusted advisor who is part of the inner circle on their client's team as I was. I want recruiters to get the respect they truly deserve! My sincere hope is that you save the years of trial and error by incorporating the strategies shared within.

What follows are the three main principles I have been sharing with my clients for years which will allow you to have a minimum 50% increase in your revenue or a double, depending on where your revenues are. If you apply the principles I share in this book and you work them daily, you will see the results.

Enjoy the Book!

I hope this book educates you and helps change your way of thinking about your recruiter business and encourages you to Double Your Placements in the next 121 Days.

To Your Success!

Michael Gionta

Principle #1: Moving from Overwhelm to Clarity...

Let's start by taking a moment and thinking about what your goal was for the last year versus where you are at today. Write those two numbers down on a piece of paper. What your goal was for the year and where you are now. Be honest with yourself. All progress starts with telling the truth.

What was your goal? You might have written, "Never really had one." That is fairly revealing, wouldn't you say? If you did have a goal for the year, compare that number to what your results are here to date. Write it down, circle it, now what has the gap? If you have exceeded your goal, what has the excess? Write that down.

This book is going to share with you how to get out of the gap and move closer to your goal. The first step in the process is to get more clarity about your business.

Principle Number One is about how to go from overwhelm to clarity. The best analogy I can give you is to imagine the power goes out in your home on a moonless night. It is completely pitch black; you have a two-story house, and the flashlight is downstairs. You want to get to the flashlight to see if it is your power box. If you get out of bed and it is pitch black, think about what that feels like and what you are doing. Put yourself in that situation. You are probably feeling for the wall and then feeling for the door. Even though you may have owned the house for 30 years, you are going to go very slowly and you are going to go tentatively.

Eventually, the power comes back on and the lights come on and you have to get downstairs. Now you can sprint. You can get there 10 times as fast as in that moment when you were surrounded by blackness.

If you have ever been to a circus or seen a circus on TV or even a cartoon of a circus, you can imagine what a lion tamer looks like. He's got two things in hand - a whip in one hand and a chair or a stool in the other.

Why would a lion tamer, when trying to tame a 1,000 pound lion, benefit from a simple four-legged stool? Here we have a 175-pound lion tamer and a 1,000 pound lion. That lion can break that stool in a heartbeat. The primary reason lion tamers use a four-legged stool and shove the stool at the lion with the legs facing the lion is because the lion tries to focus on all four legs of the stool simultaneously. As a result, he cannot be aggressive. He's sort of frozen because he doesn't just pick one leg and leap.

Hopefully, you are able to tie this together with your typical recruiter. A typical recruiter is emailing, thinking about closing deals, thinking about new business development, thinking about research, thinking about being on LinkedIn, etc.

When you are not clear on the direction you are going, you aren't going to get where you want to go. What does the extra revenue you are going to bring in mean for you? It is not just monetary either, I am talking about lifestyle.

What is that increase in revenue going to allow for you that you do not have now? Imagine I am sitting here in my white doctor's smock doing an analysis of the many situations I find when I ask somebody, "What would that level of revenue allow for you that you do not have now?" When I ask this question, I do not get clear answers.

If you look at that gap, if you look at that goal number and you are not specifically clear on what that is going to allow for you versus what you have now, it is probably one of the main reasons you have not achieved it.

In the absence of being crystal clear and passionate about something, the outcome tends to be that you make just enough placements. You have probably had that month where you made a placement or two, you excel and think, "I am good for a couple of months." When you say, "I am good for a couple of months," it doesn't mean you are on target. It means, "I am paying the bills."

A lot of us, who are paying the bills as recruiters, are very fortunate. It puts us in the top 5% or 10% of income earners nationwide, but it is not what you <u>really</u> wanted. I am going to challenge you to get clear on what reaching your bigger goal allows for you.

When my daughter was younger, I remember a rainy weekend day and we were going to do a puzzle together. We dumped all the pieces of the puzzle onto the table. Think about it for a moment. What has one of the first things you do when you sit down to do a puzzle? No, it is not starting with the edges; not looking for the corners; not turning all the pieces over. Those are all tactics and good ones. The first thing you do when you sit down to do a puzzle is you look at the box top. What are you going to make? What has the big picture? What has it going to look like when done?

I would challenge you that most of you reading this do not know what your business looks like done. You do not have a box top. I am going to help you create your box top, so you know what your business looks like when it is done.

Too often, we get caught up in billings. Back to that question I asked earlier, what would those excess billings that you are not getting now allow for you that you do not have now?

What I found is, I always thought recruiters were highly materialistic. You'd be surprised how many times I hear people say they want financial security but they have not defined what financial security looks like for them. They want a smooth financial retirement. I ask them, "What does that look like for you?" They answer, "I won't have to worry about money." I tell them, "Take the time to sit down with a financial planner then and define what that number looks like for you."

We all have different life situations and desires. Do you want to be living in Florida for the winter? Do you want to be traveling in an RV? There is no right or wrong answer here, except to not have an answer.

I will challenge you to figure out what that answer looks like for you. Is it extra material things? Is it elimination of debt? Is it a combination of all of those things? Write down what it looks like for you. What has your box top? You should incorporate friends, family, personal financial situation, professional situation, relationship with your clients, etc.

Ask yourself, why did you want to become an entrepreneur in the first place? What was your vision? What have you compromised? Because maybe you have told yourself, "It is too hard." The biggest mistake I made as a coach when I started doing this in 2007 was skipping this step. I just jumped into here's how to get retainers, here's some scripts and templates on getting searches when you can get a close, engage and where you can up your revenue. Like a lot of people, I went straight to tactics.

I was getting OK results. But when I started implementing these steps with my clients, I saw my results take off because we were able to connect the tactical with the emotional. I think we are all taught in this business, "You have to be on the phone," to the point where you do not do smart things like go to conferences such as NAPS or the Fordyce Forum.

I had a client who had this fantastic dog and would take it to a local senior center. To do this, she was sneaking out to go to the senior center on a few Friday afternoons to be with seniors to give something back. She enjoyed it, the dog enjoyed it, and the seniors loved it. I asked her, "Why don't we engineer your week so that you build more in 4 1/2 days per week to hit your billing goal, and then you can liberate yourself so you can go Friday afternoons guilt free; no more sneaking out. That is exactly what happened.

What is the equivalent for you?

Additionally, I have clients, two brothers who are partners who also felt like that. They felt like they always had to be in the office. I asked them what it would look like if they could bill more and then in the summer, be able to take Fridays off to golf. Again, we engineered their week to make this happen. The result? They were more productive in four days than in the 5 previous unfocussed days!

The key is, bill more, work less. What would that look like for you? Really stop and think about it for a moment.

I have another client, who is president of a large national charitable organization. He travels all over the world. He doubled his billings so he could increase his travel time and service to the organization. It is all possible, but the key for each client was they each got more focused on the right things in the business. When they were physically at their desk and in their office, they were getting more done because these were things they were passionate about. The common denominator was they built significantly more placements, up to twice as many, which allowed them to follow what they were very passionate about.

When I got clear about these questions myself I was able to coach baseball in the spring, and in the fall. Furthermore, I began to grow my own coaching business.

My personal business was allowing more time for that, which revitalized me to do better coaching and better mentorship. When I was at a desk and running an office, I was a better owner because I was able to clear my head of recruiting for a few hours a few times a week. That is the benefit of it, stopping and getting clarity for yourself.

If you could develop 50% or even double your billings, what does that liberate for you personally and professionally? I want you to stop reading right now and write that down. Get specific here.

If you could increase billings by 50%, what does that liberate for you personally and professionally?

Then ask yourself, "Why are you denying yourself that now? Why are you compromising on your ideal life?"

The first key to doubling revenue is gaining clarity. These exercises are to help you get clear on your goals, which is the first key step.

Here are the TOP 3 Things that a 50% to 100% increase would allow for me personally:

1)

2)

3)

Principle #2: Moving from Roller Coaster Revenue to Predictable Income...

Principle Number Two is going from roller coaster revenue to predictable income. A lot of people, when I have met with them face to face, say to me, "Hey, Mike. All I need to do is just to focus more. I need to be more disciplined. I just need to focus on making more placements. If I focus on making more placements, I will make more placements."

This could not be more wrong! **Chasing placements is an emotional nightmare.**

If you think about it, the placement is the one thing in the process of what we do as recruiters that we cannot control. Can we influence it? Absolutely. Can we increase the likelihood of it? Yes, through our expertise, through our knowledge, and through building our interaction with clients. You know that already. There's nothing you can do that can change the person who emotionally freaks out at the last minute and decides, after they have taken the offer, that they are not going to take it. There's nothing you can do to control a last-minute merger or acquisition hiring freeze.

Those are all outside of your realm of control. Yet, when those things happen, we naturally get frustrated. If you look back over the last year, how many placements have you counted on that you thought were done deals that "blew up"? It is going to happen every year. The mistake we make is, we focus on the placement, we focus on the one thing we can not control.

Principle Number Two, going from roller coaster revenue to predictable income, requires us to understand exactly what needs to happen every year, every quarter, every week, and every day in your business.

I will give you some examples. First, look at that goal number you wrote down in the previous chapter. Maybe now you are going to change it. Hopefully you are going to change it because my gut feeling is your original goal number probably did not have enough meaning behind it.

Let's assume for argument's sake that you have defined a goal and it is $300,000 a year in personal billings and that your average fee is $25,000. The average fee in the industry is somewhere between $20,000-25,000 as this book was written.

If your goal is to do $300,000, there are probably going to be months where you are going to bill nothing. Even if you do everything correctly, you most likely will blank some months

I will bet thousands of dollars on that for most of you. Additionally, there could be a month you bill $100,000. That again is something you can not control.

What you can control is what goes on at your desk every day. Your goal number may be different than the $300,000. It is one of the things I am always working on with my clients. Once we dial into what their goal number is, the billing number they are truly committed to we can engineer EXACTLY what needs to happen for them to achieve this.

Please understand, there is an *exact number of interviews that need to be arranged every month, every week for you to hit $300,000.* You are going to know you are on target next week once you dial in that number.

To achieve arranging those interviews, there is a precise number of candidates you need to speak with to get one interview arranged. I have measured this with all my recruiters and dozens and dozens of clients. I have never seen people who measure their metrics not get within 5% of the billings we predicted.

The key to get off the roller coaster revenue ride and into predictable income is to know what those numbers are for you. Start tracking marketing presentations, recruiting presentations, first time interviews, submittals, and of course, placements and revenue.

- Recruit Presentation = a LIVE conversation with a potential recruit on an assignment you have to fill. Voice mails and emails do NOT count.

- Marketing Presentations are LIVE conversations with prospects in an attempt to get a search assignment. These are also conversations with existing clients to get more business.

- First time interviews are phone conversations OR facet to face meetings that occur for the first time with your client. (I do not count second interviews as they don't increase my ability to predict placements).

- A submittal is how many people you are presenting to a client on an existing job order.

- Placements and revenue need no definition!

Additionally you need to know what the relationships to those numbers are, meaning the key ratios. The ratios will show you how many recruit presentations you need to get first time interview. They will show you how many marketing presentations you need to take a search assignment.

Once you dial into those metrics, you will also know how many interviews it takes to make a placement.

THIS IS THE KEY METRIC TO PREDICTING YOUR BILLINGS AND TO CREATING PREDICTABLE INCOME!!!

If your goal is one placement a month and you know how many interviews it takes to make one placement, then you divide that by four. That is how many interviews you have to arrange every week and how many candidates you have to talk to and you divide that by four weeks, and you get how many people you have to talk to every week. It is literally that simple but people do not track numbers because they think that they "do not have the time."

If you are not tracking metrics, imagine you are an archer. If you are going out into competition every day into a foggy field where you can not see the target. You are just firing arrows in the general direction with no feedback mechanism. Meaning, you do not even know if you are on target. Every once in a while, somebody off in the distance yells "Bulls eye!" You are flinging arrows left and right and just randomly going after the target. That is what my days looked like in recruiting until I figured out this key strategy.

For people who are doing business this way, when you are not clear on exactly, specifically and precisely what you have to do to hit your revenue target my guess is that your activity is not close to what you need to hit your goal. You might be looking at LinkedIn profiles, doing the research so that you call the right people.

I am seeing people invest anywhere from 2-5 hours a day doing their own research to find the "right people to call". They are doing a $15 an hour task which can easily be outsourced to someone else who is probably better at it than they are.

There are places that have researchers available for hire on a per hour basis such as Elance and oDesk. If you post the job the right way and you post to hire a researcher, I have seen rates range anywhere from $8 to $20 an hour. If you find the right person in the right way, you can get 200 to 300 names, contact information, email addresses, phone numbers for $50 or $100.

You are going to have to kiss some frogs to find your "prince" in this process. You are going to have to likely hire a few people to get through to the right one.

This is not like hiring people in the traditional sense. They get $50 or $100 dollars to conduct a trial. If they do not do well and they are way off target, you do not give them anymore projects. It is that simple.

The reason people do activities and tasks like this is they are not clear on what it takes to be widely productive in this business. Also, if they are doing research they can fool themselves into the belief that they are truly busy and really working hard!

If you are going to bill $300,000 a year, this roughly represents a bill rate of around $200 an hour. Every hour you do your own research, every hour you try to figure things out for yourself, I want you to imagine writing a check for $185 to the business. Meaning at your $200 an hour bill rate, minus $15 you could have paid a researcher. You are writing a $185 check out of your future accounts receivable for every hour you do your own research. Every hour you do this is money you lose forever!

I say that because some of you out there are thinking you are actually saving money. It is actually just the opposite! This is probably one of the most expensive things you can do. I generally find figuring things out for yourself is one of the most expensive things anyone can do. It is one of the reasons I have always had mentors in my life. I have always found somebody who got to a higher level quicker than me, cut them a check, and had them teach me how they did it.

I did it when I was recruiting. I have two mentors in coaching right now. One of the things that you notice about me is I am able to provide an entirely different solution than most of the other trainers in the industry. No knock on them, they have great techniques, but I am not a trainer. I do not own a website with a million videos. I actually refer my clients to those trainers for "training". People come to me when they want help getting the training implemented and installed in their recruiting business.

In summary, principle Number Two requires you to dial into exactly, specifically, precisely what has to occur every quarter, every month, every week, and every day in your business.

Make sure you also factor in your vacation time. There are 13 weeks in a quarter. You are not going to say you are going to have 52 weeks in a year because I do not think any of you are going to work 52 weeks a year. Factor a 46 or 48-week year when you set your goals and then do your math.

Here's another thing you could do to really ramp up productivity. Voicemails and cold calls to new clients are almost worthless. It didn't always used to be this way. As technology evolves we see fewer and fewer prospects returning cold voice mails.

I do not care what the quality is. I do not want to say stop doing them for those of you who are recruiters who report to an owner. I am saying if this was visual and we threw up a chart of return call rates from 1990 to now, you will see the steady decline in return call percentage rates. So, how do you fix this?

One thing that we have been doing remarkably well in our office and with my clients is email marketing of great candidates directly to the hiring managers. Not a mass email, but very short benefit oriented emails. The key with these emails is to not engage the prospect in an email dialogue. Their response might be something like, *"Send me a resume. Tell me a little bit about them. What do they make? Where do they live?"* If you answer that question in an email, you are probably going to find it very difficult to move the process forward. You want to use that email to get them on the phone. Use their response to get them on the phone. Those are warm leads.

By doing that, we have been able to really ramp up the number of marketing presentations especially to the people who are quasi-raising their hands say, "I might have an opening." That is a quick technique you can do.

Principle Number Two is to know exactly, specifically, and precisely what those things look like. When most people come to me initially, their activity is generally too low to justify the level of billings they want. Most also had no idea what the "right" activity for them was in the first place!

Once you dial in to what the right activity for you and your recruiting office is much of the mystery of this business will disappear! With many of you it is probably a 40-50% bump in most of your activity levels, maybe doubling or sometimes, in extreme situations, even more.

Principle #3: Moving from Transactional Vendor to Trusted Advisor...

Principle Number Three is going from annoying flash transactional vendor to trusted advisor. Let's look at why this really occurs in our industry right now. Let's just be honest with each other. That is not really your fault. We are all trained the same way. When we are all trained the same way, what happens? We all sound alike. Our presentations sound alike.

Sometimes, we make calls like a check-in call, "Hey, Bob, I am just checking in to see if you need any open job requirements filled?" Then we ask ourselves, "Why can not I get a retainer on a call like that?" WHY?? That call and that recruiter sounds like a used car salesman. I hate this word so I am going to use it here: pitch. You are making a completely unsophisticated PITCH!

When you are pitching, you are not consultative, you are not in the trusted advisor mode. Think about it. When someone said consultant, when someone said trusted advisor, what do they know? They know your situation, which is why you can rely on them.

Let's use your financial advisor as an example. How do they get to know your situation? They did not get to know your situation by coming to you and saying, "Hey, you know what? I can get you 20% returns a year and I can help you hit your retirement goals."

No. They ask questions like, "Where are you at in your life? How do you define a successful retirement? What does that look like for you?" Even some of those questions I asked you to consider earlier are examples that trusted advisors ask versus just trying to get the deal done.

One of the things that prevents us from becoming a trusted advisor is our presentations in the recruiting industry are mostly all the same. We take searches the same way. We are going to call, and the prospect says, *"Oh yeah, you know, before we get going, what has your fee?"* If you answer that question, you are dead in the water in becoming a trusted advisor. Know for yourself that you are going to enter commodity-based dialogue. Because now, the dialogue is about the fee and then you are going to try to say, "Well, the reason we charge more, you will say 30%, they will say we only pay you 18%." You will have a conversation and you are compromised at ..... 18%!!!

Because right now, they are looking at you like they are looking at a gallon of gas. Gas is around $3.50 a gallon in your neighborhood but you know two blocks away, you can get it for $2.50. Why would you pay $3.50 a gallon when you just have to drive two more blocks to get it for $2.50? That is what the perception of recruiters in the marketplace is. *"Why would I pay Joe Recruiter, 28% or 30% when I have got all these people who have agreed to 18%?"*

I am not agreeing with the sentiment. I am just saying it is what most prospects think because of the terrible way we often present ourselves to them. The prospect looks at that as a gap of, *"Why would I pay more when all of you recruiters all have access to pretty much the same bodies,"* which is what they think.

Prospects also think that using multiple recruiters increases the likelihood of filling their job because they have access to multiple and different databases. We all know if you do a search the right way that perception is false. We can not, however, just tell them they are wrong. We have to ask them questions like, *"Is it your perception that using three or four recruiters increases the likelihood of filling this three to four times? Yes. Are you open to an argument where the opposite might be true?"*

At this point you can walk them through a detailed description of what doing a real search is like and how you will expose the prospect to many more people than they would be exposed to if they had just a few people doing a quick database search for a lower fee and with no real commitment to the project or to the prospect.

Before we go to a solution here on becoming a trusted advisor, it is really important that you understand why you are being treated like this. Most recruiters do not make the time or money to invest in themselves. They are running off executing the same mediocre and failed strategies over and over again waiting and praying to divinely be granted great clients who pay high fees with money up front.

These are the same recruiters that are answering the question, "Hey, before we get started, what has your fee?" They answer it and they agree to that 18%. Remember, **NEVER quote a fee at the beginning of a conversation. Never, never, never!**

Once the commodity based recruiter has already agreed to the 18%, they ask incredibly sophisticated questions like, *"Why do not you tell me what you are looking for? What are your duties and responsibilities? What are the four biggest selling points of your company?"*

Again, there's nothing wrong with those questions. It is just that there are about 80,257 people asking them that question every time they have an opening. If they have had a career in 20 years of management, they have heard those same questions over and over and over and over again.

In that vein, if you are going to be treated differently, you have to sound different. Does this make sense?

If you want to be treated like a trusted advisor, you need to invest the time and the resources to become a trusted advisor first. That means reengineering the entire client and candidate approach. Don't let this intimidate you as you can do this over time with practice and the right mentor.

When I start taking a search, here is my favorite opening question to start the process, *"I want you to imagine as we get started here, I want you to imagine you have hired this person for X role and a year from now, you are walking down the hall and you are thinking, 'My gosh, this person, this guy, this gal, has had an outstanding first year.' Can you tell me what they have accomplished?"*

When you ask a question like this, you take the prospect to the visual part of their brain. When you take them to the visual part of their brain, they actually do imagine what has happened, and they will give you an entirely different answer. They will actually give you a three-dimensional answer. What is that question a substitute for? That question is a substitute for what are the duties and the responsibilities. Trust me, when you go out and test this in the market, when my clients test this, it sets the tone for the whole conversation. You want to do that with every question in a search assignment.

I used to keep a thesaurus by my desk and I used to change the words. The key here is where can you take them as often as possible? You set the keyword, imagine, to the visual part of their brain to change the questions you are asking. Because if you are going to get trusted advisor status and high fees with your clients, you need to go from that "annoying vendor" status to sounding like a consultant, a really good consultant.

If you think of somebody coming out of a nationally known consulting company, they are going to go in to a company and they are going to do a really good analysis of their client's situation before they go to a solution or a prescription for their problems. I am not talking about fees and I am not talking about my process. I am talking about 25 minutes, 30 minutes into the call when I have exhausted myself to discovering their situation, the selling points for their opportunity. Why someone that is currently happily employed is even going to be intrigued by this whatsoever?

Something else you can do to help become a trusted advisor is to develop your ideal client avatar. This leads me to discuss another mistake I see recruiters make is they believe great clients are found. Actually, I used to think the same thing.

Here is what I have learned. Great clients are not found. Great clients are made. I remember I had a client and they were fantastic, textbook great client, great fees, great process, and great turnaround time. I remember thinking, *"Why can not more of my clients be like this one?"* This was early in my career. Then I asked myself the question again with a different tone, "Why CAN'T my clients be like this?" I asked myself, "What is it about this relationship that makes it tick?"

I looked at my ideal client avatar, what I was going to aspire to with these kind of fees was a deposit-based search with access to the hiring manager. A lot of these situations by the way, to have trusted advisor status, involve human resources. With most of my best clients, HR was intricately involved in managing the relationship but hands off with my ability to communicate with the hiring managers. This is how to use Human Resources in the right strategic way so that you are reporting into them with the data that you are getting so that they are not insecure about what value you are actually providing their organization.

The best place to look to target some of these future client avatars is probably people that are paying terrible fees with terrible terms right now. Why? Because there is a huge talent shortage in this economy. More than likely, the hiring managers in those companies are incredibly frustrated with their existing recruiting operations.

I would challenge you to start putting together those lists of types of prospects I just mentioned above. Look to target companies where you have typically thought:

"I am not calling those people. They only pay 15%. I am not calling those people. They want a six month money back guarantee." All those prospects that you have not talked to in a month, start targeting them, and start doing the right type of analysis with them.

Ask them questions about what, if anything, has going wrong in their ability to attract talent. If they have had challenges ask some great questions that expose them to the ramifications of leaving those positions open any longer.

Next, put together a strong proposal as to how you would be different and also show how the structure of the relationship would also be different to solve the problem the other recruiters could not under their existing structure. If they say (and they WILL), *"Well, we only have 37 people who have approved that fee."* I say, "Well, I thought you wanted to fix that because you just told me you are frustrated?"

Answer this for yourself right now: what keeps you in the transaction zone? What are the things you are doing? No progress in your life starts without telling the truth to yourself. What are some of the things that keep you in the transaction zone? What are the consequences for you not changing your approach? If you look 12 months out from now and you do not change anything, where are you going to be a year from now? What are those client relationships going to be like?

Principle Number Three is knowing what you need to change and improve on your approach from a diagnostic and questioning standpoint. Go through your search assignment forms and change the questions. You want to find the same information but how can you ask those same questions consultatively? I gave you a few different examples. That is the first trigger.

The second step is putting together a list of companies that are in your niche that maybe have had the worst financial terms. Are you going to convert all of them? No, of course not! If you convert one out of 10 or 20, that is going to be fantastic. Because once you convert a client like this you will often get MULTIPLE openings because you were the only one who could deliver great talent to them on a consistent basis.

Many of these first assignments will be you testing them and them testing you to see if you are truly worth the premium in fees and terms. I used to use this phrase, "Let's work on this one thing as a beta project to see if the look and feel is different for you and if our process makes sense, you will hire our guy and you will pay a little bit more but we will have done what the other recruiters could not accomplish. If it makes sense, we could talk about expanding this into other positions in the organization."

Implementation...
Putting the Principles in Place...

Here's a little coaching exercise based on what you have heard that will help you get some clarity so that you can have some specific takeaways and actions to perform.

All progress starts by telling the truth, so we are going to do a little truth-telling exercise. Get out a blank piece of paper and draw three columns, a column on the far left and the far right, and a column in the middle. We are going to do an exercise called 'From This to This.' I actually do this with my clients. You are getting something for free that is probably one of the tool I receive the best feedback from my paid clients and I thought I would share that with you because it can be done quickly to help give you some clarity.

Think about right now and look back over the last 90 days. Write about your monthly billings. You are going to put that in the far left column that is "From This." Write about your monthly billings over the last 90 days. No excuses, just EXACTLY what those billings are.

Write about your team. A lot of you might be solo recruiters. Is it just you? Write about your researcher. Do you have one? Write about what your day looks like right now. If it is a plan, is it organized, is it reactive?

Write about your reputation in your niche? Do people know you well enough to pick up the phone and give you a call, more than one or two companies?

Write about your existing client relationships, people you have agreements with. Are you a trusted advisor? Are you in that commodity transactional zone? Write about the quality of those client relationships; again, not what they are going to be, write about these relationships as they exist now.

Write about your metrics. Do you track them at all? Are they helping you keep accurate billing predictions or is it something you have grown up with in this business thinking it was a punishment?

Actually, when you track the right metrics, a lot of times, you will find what activities you have to make less of.

Write about your free time. What is going on right now? Are you doing all the things you want to do not just necessarily vacation-wise with your family but giving back? Is giving back something you are going to get to later or has it been something you are getting to now? Again, I could go deeper but these are the big trigger points to go along with the three points we have talked about.

Now, I want you to go to the far right column. You are going to fill in the far right column now. *Imagine it is 12 months from now, a year from this date.* You and I bump into each other at a conference someplace, on the street, wherever and you say to me, *"Mike, I am really thrilled with my progress over the last 12 months. I can not believe this. Let me tell you what has happened!"*

The key here is happy with your progress. Twelve months from now, if you are going to be really happy with your progress, I am going to ask you these questions:

- How do you want your billings to be different over those 12 months? How is that different 12 months from now?

- Write about your team. Have you added researchers? Maybe if you are billing a lot, you are adding part-time virtual recruiters to help you fill it.

- Write about what your day looks like 12 months from now? Tell me what your week looks like.

- Write about how your reputation has changed in your niche. Were you happy with your progress? Again, not done but gosh, these things are so cool they happened in the last 12 months.

- Write about your clients. Tell me about how you got a trusted advisor status with more of them maybe.

- Write about the quality of your relationships. What are they doing with you in 12 months that they are not doing today?

- Write about how you can predict your income now. Tell me what you have put in place to track for the right numbers.

- Write about your work-life balance a year from now.

- What are the things you have been putting off doing for a long time that you finally got done in the last 12 months. Write about that relative you have reached out. Tell me about that vacation you took. Tell me about that weekend you took that you have been,

"Nah, It is too expensive. I can not get time away from the office." Tell me about what happened.

Here's what I know, 90% of your goals are 100% doable in the next 12 months. My guess is, many of these goals have been on your list for some time and they have just got rolled forward and rolled forward and rolled forward. Now, we are going to look at why.

In the middle column, we are going to look at what has slowing you down, getting in the way or stopping you from getting what you want.

- In terms of what has holding you back, right now, what has been your mindset? What do you do that sabotages yourself every month, every week, and every day?

- Right now, what gets in the way as it relates to your planning? Is it done consistently? Is it done daily?

- Write about your ability right now to get retained or engaged searches. What holds you back from having these great client relationships?

- What gets in the way of your productivity? The only thing you should be doing all day long is candidly talking to clients and closing deals: closing deals all day long, but engaging people to take searches, engaging people to assess them in their careers, in their appropriateness, and then putting those things together to the point of an offer. Everything outside of that is productive, but probably can be outsourced.

What gets in the way of your productivity? What gets in the way of one of the things we talked about, hiring a researcher, if you do not already have one or two? I probably challenge you by two or three, because it is a variable, not a fixed cost. On a scale of 1-10, where are you in your trusted advisor status with your current client? A 10 being 'I fill almost every opening, maybe not in their company but through the division I work in. I am the go-to person'; and one is 'I do not ever talk to anybody and I get emailed openings. I submit emailed resumes and when I make a placement, I do an emailed invoice.' Where are you on that spectrum?

- What are the things right now that hold you back from being a 10?

- What holds you back from keeping really good numbers so you can predict your revenue so that you can know exactly, specifically and precisely what needs to happen today or tomorrow in your office, at your desk, so that you hit whatever that billing target is you outlined at the beginning of the book?

- Lastly, if I were to follow you around in your office for a day or two with a clipboard, what would I see? What would I tell you to stop doing? What would I tell you to do differently?

Everything in that middle column you just wrote, that is what I help my clients fix. Those are the problems I eat for breakfast.

I am not quite sure why you are reading this book. It could be because you are bored, overwhelmed, and not clear on what a great solo recruiting operation should look like and what things you should be doing to maximize your productivity on a day-to-day or week-to-week basis. Maybe you are frustrated because you do not know exactly, specifically, and precisely what you need to do every day and every week? Or it could be because you saw 'trusted advisor' and you are caught in an internal recruiter, HR hell, and have low paying and non-responsive clients?

If this sounds at all like you I invite you to consider getting help and to stop trying to do everything on your own.

I invested years of my life and hundreds of thousands of dollars in doing recruiting and the recruiting business the wrong way until, through a lot of practice, trial and error I began to master the three key principles I discussed in this book.

To get help installing these principles in your firm please keep reading!

Here's How the Double Your Revenue in 121 Days or Less Program Works...

I am giving you the steps that must be implemented right away to increase your revenue by at least 50% or even 100%. You need to invest some quiet time and get clear on how this business serves you and how to engineer your time and your practice, to allow more life in your life. Sitting at your desk, checking your email every 2.5 seconds, your fantasy football or baseball teams, how the stock market is doing every four or five minutes is not a good, fun way to invest 8 to 10 hours a day at your desk. I encourage you to continue measuring the right numbers and the right ratios to keep you on course, and outsource those $5-15 an hour activities like research.

I can honestly promise you that many prospect companies are looking for trusted advisors as search partners. Remember, great clients are made. They are not found. You need to invest your time and have the right scripts. You need to reengineer that initial approach to the client. You need to reengineer the way you take searches. That brings up the obvious question: How do I continue to get these results in my business or how do I get these results in my business? You could do it fast OR you could do it slow. It is your choice.

The slowest way to get anything done is by trial and error, especially trial and error without a feedback mechanism. Who's going to see your blind spots? It is not just the slowest; it is actually the most expensive. You see, every month you are not executing, if you look at that gap number you wrote at the beginning of the book and you divide that by 12, That is what it has cost you in lost placements, lost revenue, revenue you do not actually see, invoices you never typed. Look at that goal number. Look at your actual number. My guess is that gap has been there. This isn't the first time.

Einstein said, "Problems cannot be solved by the same mind that created them."

I have been helping solo owners with these very same frustrating challenges for the past several years. I recently completely reengineered my mentoring system to make it more accessible to more recruiters. It is called *How to Double Your Placements and Double Your Revenue in 121 Days or Less*. It is an A to Z, nuts and bolts system that teaches you and supports you through these three major shifts:

- How to go from overwhelmed to clarity,
- How to go from roller coaster revenue to predictable income, and,
- How to go from annoying transactional vendor to trusted advisor.

The program allows you to significantly increase your revenue by 50% to 100% ***without working longer hours.***

Bluntly, this program is not for everyone because there is no magic to it. I am not going to come to your office and bless you and you are going to instantly start performing on this stuff. I wish I could. I can help you make a lot more money. You need to simply invest the time to put the things I tell you in place and make it cut and paste. We have the templates for the scripts and the tools.

It is also not right for the person who feels life isn't being fair to them and who is always looking to the outside world for their success.

Again, I designed this program to help people get out of overwhelm, to remove the mystery of how to sustain high-level billings, and to stop being treated like a transactional vendor. The Double Your Placements Mentoring Program will get you clarity by taking you through some step-by-step exercises where we are going to have time, spend 90 minutes giving you the right questions that frankly, many of my clients say were invaluable in moving them forward.

We are also going to crack the code and go deeper on this. Throughout the program, as you change and evolve and as you start billing more, other plateaus and other opportunities are going to open up to you and you are probably going to want even more out of yourself.

Right away, month one, we start by giving you three specific strategies for marketing without cold calling. Because of the changing dynamics of voicemail, it is becoming harder and harder to get through to your prospects. This one technique alone will pay for the entire program ten times over as you get ahold of more clients who give you warm leads to follow-up on. Then I teach you how to convert them into exclusive and/or engaged clients.

In addition, I am going to teach you what it took me years of trial and error to learn on what hiring managers really think and how to turn those around so that you are a partner, again, not an annoying vendor.

Again, I spend 90 minutes alone on teaching you how to take great search. NO ONE is teaching this process right now. It is a highly consultative approach and mirrors how consultants go after business versus how recruiting firms go after business. It has transformed not only the way I was able to get clients on a much more exclusive retainer basis, but it is reflected in my clients' successes also now. It is one thing you'd say, "Mike, you have done it." Now, It is been repeated over and over and over again by my clients in this program. Most of the clients I begin working with who are serious about this start getting retainers where they have never gotten them before just by "filling in the numbers" with my process.

I have had a client, who was in the business 30 years, plodding along and little bit stuck. Within 14 months, her business was 85% engaged.

Furthermore, in the Double Your Placements Mentoring Program, we start getting you clear, measuring the right numbers. I am going to give you all the templates so you have the right, exact, specific, precise target to pursue.

At the same time, we begin measuring the right metrics so you know, again, what has to happen on your desk every day, every week, and every month to double your performance and your revenue generation. It is not working necessarily twice as hard. I will provide you with an Online Metrics Tool and teach you how to use it. Now there is no excuse not to track your key metrics. Just log into the tool and enter your numbers. We have a full training on how to use it and we also have coaching calls each month to support any questions you have on metrics.

Additionally, you are going to learn an easy system to outsource research with the templates, how to post your ad, how to find the researches, how to vet them, how to set expectations with them so that we can liberate three or four hours a day for you to invest in candidate and client acquisition.

Also you will learn to master the art of getting a retainer and engagement fee. One engagement fee by the way, and your entire investment of the program for the whole year is covered. When you have engaged clients, for those of you who already have them, you know they get back to you. Getting a hold of them is not really a big problem.

As the program goes on, we are going to get into advanced business development strategies, client retention strategies, allowing you to build off the momentum of the early part of the program.

All the calls are going to be recorded and put up on our private membership site. New content is going to be covered each month so you can implement one or two ideas slowly and master them. I do not want to overwhelm you with new ideas, so we layer them in slowly throughout the year.

In the group mentoring program, we have three calls a month, one or two content training calls and one or two, depending on the month, coaching, implementation, support calls. This is where you get me live on a call. In those calls, because it is a smaller group, you get to come in with your challenges that might be getting you stuck on moving forward.

We also have a private Facebook group when you join the program. You are going to see over a year's worth of great content (on all of the above topics and more) you can go through on people's questions and my answers. Search by topic and you will see some great ideas you can use right away in your business.

I usually comment on these posts daily so there is coaching in between the coaching calls. I am generally in that private Facebook group and the only people that can see it are my clients in this program. You get answers to a ton of problems so you can get instant value because as soon as you sign up, you can join that Facebook group.

I have charged as much as $1,000 a month or $12,000 a year to access the same content I have described in a very similar environment. One of the things I did some time ago, with some great coaching, was determine how I can provide this similar, if not better, value at a lower investment to impact more people's revenue.

By structuring in the way I have done with the membership site and access to the calls that are recorded and putting together slightly larger groups, I was able to lower the investment down to only $397 a month. You can also go to **www.therecruiteru.com/solo** to access and enroll in the Solo Mentoring Program... *Double Your Placements, Double Your Revenue in 121 Days or Less!!*

I had a testimonial from someone who joined my program some time ago. In this program and structure I am talking about, she achieved her 12 month goal in ONLY seven months, which was double the revenue over her previous year!

I am one of those "trust but verify" guys myself. Go to my LinkedIn page, Mike Gionta, and look at what other people have to say. Nick Mancino, if you look at what he said, *"Mike made us a promise, if you do exactly what I tell you to do, you will get the exact results and he delivered."* That is a member of the Double Your Placements Program. There are 15 or 20 testimonials of people who all got the exact result.

The results are going to vary based on your effort. This is a 12-month program and I expect people who are passionately committed to their success. I do not want any dabblers in this. However, some of you might say, "I like the concept. Will Mike deliver?" But you are not sure. What I am going to do, because again, I am confident **that if you do the work**, you are going to see the results. I am going to ask you to make a two-month commitment to the program. Enroll in the program for two months. If it is not what I am promising you here, if you are not seeing results, you can opt out anywhere between Day 60 and Day 90. If you terminate your membership between months two and three, and we'll part friends, no questions asked. I may call you up. I may send you just a quick note for your feedback as to what we could also improve.

I could tell you, from my past experience, that almost ALL of the people that have dropped over the time since we started this, were simply not doing the work. I want to give you that no questions asked 60-90 day window to work with my material. If you hang out for the three months, you are making a commitment to the program for a year. Then after 12 months, it is month to month. After 12 months, you can opt out with 30 days' notice any time you want, because I have got more than a one-year curriculum for those that want to continue to work with me on growing their revenues, growing the quality of their client relationships and growing their free time away from work.

I want you to imagine... you are going to work with me for a year, based on the strategies outlined and that you have read in this book. Imagine what that will do for you and your business... for your quality of LIFE! If you think after doing this work and following my blueprint you are not going to make at least one more placement, at say about $20,000 know that at even this LOW level of expectation that this **represents a 4 to 1 return on YOUR investment!** If you hang out for the whole year, your investment is $4,800 if you make one placement. Now, if you are in this to make just one placement, you probably do not have the right motivation to be here. I would challenge you, with your goals and aspiration, to add six figures *minimum* to your billings without working longer and harder. I can work you through that challenge on the coaching calls and in the Facebook group.

The link for more details and to enroll is **www.therecruiteru.com/solo**. In addition I am going to include an extra $1,000 in bonus materials that you can use right away. It will be available digitally. You will see it on the membership site. As soon as you enroll, you are going to get a user name and a password to the membership site. You will see the Recruiting Masters Section where I have interviewed people like Greg Doersching, Craig Millard on *How to Build the Million Dollar Desk*. There are about 12 modules on different training to get you motivated and off to a quick start. As soon as you enroll, you can download the material in the Recruiting Masters area.

Here's the Most Common Questions Recruiters Have About Our Coaching Program...

When will the next coaching program get started? We are always starting a new program. There will be three coaching calls every month.

Is there any contract to sign? No. Here's what I am going to do. Like I said, if people do not want to be there, I do not want them there in my program. However, I am huge on the term commitment. I am asking for a two-month minimum commitment. After the two months, what I am asking you to do is between months two and three, if you are not getting the value, simply send us a note. We'll stop the billing and discontinue the membership no questions asked. Honestly, the reason I do this is because I want someone committed to success. If they know they can bail quickly, my experience with those people is they always have an out. If $397 a month is a lot of money, then this ain't the right program for you.

Is there one to one coaching in this program? No, this program does not have one to one. I call it unlimited one-to-one coaching on my group calls. I generally hang out, for the most part, with an asterisk. I usually try to make it that I do not schedule anything right after it so I can be there with you guys and handle all your issues until you are done asking questions. I do not limit people on the number of questions they can ask.

For those that do want one to one, send us a note at info@therecruiteru.com at the Peak Performer Group. It is by application only. For that, I am really looking at a minimum of about $275,000 in production because those groups are mostly alumni of this program or people that are already executing at a very, very high level. Peak Performers have access to all the material I am talking about in this program. In addition, it has a one-to-one aspect. It is a smaller group. Peak members have two mastermind meetings every year, where we do two-day closed door workshops in setting specific targets, and a monthly boardroom accountability call. Just a little bit tighter relationship with me, along with significantly larger investment by you. For those who are building higher, just because you asked about one to one, send us a note, info@thetherecruiteru.com. We'll send you an application and then we can have a no-obligation call to see if or how it is appropriate for you.

I own an office with a few recruiters is this program appropriate for me and will it teach me how to hire recruiters? This program is really about working with Solo Recruiters to build their personal billings. I run other programs specifically engineered to help owners like you hire great recruiters, get them up and running quickly, make them big billers and retain them! Send me a note at mike@theRecruiterU.com to inquire about this program.

Do you still own a staffing firm or manage your own desk? No. I sold my firm a few years ago. This is all I do 100% of the time. I work with two types of owners. One, solo operators on significantly growing their revenue and I work with owners and help them systemize their business hires and onboard great recruiters and help them build teams. I teach an entirely different hiring model. Those are two different types of groups.

Metrics are my weakness. I do not know what to count in terms of interviews. Do I count on-site interviews only? HR, phone, screens, all of them, I always counted all of them as first time interviews. That might inflate your number a little bit, but as long as you are consistent. I counted all phone interviews, HR interviews. I did not have a lot of HR interviews as first interviews because that is the commodity that we want you to get you out of. In your situation, I would still start counting those because they are still highly predictive ultimately in revenue.

Where do we find these researches you were speaking about? Elance.com, oDesk.com, and there's a whole screening and vetting process. You are probably going to have to hire 8 to 10 to find a great one but there's a way to go through them quickly when you give them the right specifications. My clients are having great results. They do take some coaching by the way because when you get a list from them, you want to say, "These names and these contacts information are exactly what I am looking and here's why. Because they have this background, they compete with these company. These are off, and here's why they are off."

How do we eliminate HR as the keeper from the hiring manager? You have to provide incredible, consultative value at the front end of the process with the hiring manager. When the hiring manager says, "Go to HR," I always say, "I have no problem going to HR. Let me ask you, what happens when they do not return my call?" They will laugh. Or I will say, "What did I do to offend you?" Again, you can not do this without doing a really good diagnostic because they are just going to blow you off. They are going to go, "You are going to HR because that is where everyone else goes." I can say, without using these words, "I am not going HR because I am different." You have got this problem, you have just said this position has been open.

This is actually how I would say it, "You want me to go to Human Resources, yet you said this position has been open for three months. You are not seeing anything and you are asking me to mimic the process that you have already defined as failing," at least in this instance. Isn't that Einstein's definition of insanity, doing the same thing over and over again, expecting different results? Mr. Hiring Manager, I know HR is part of the process. I am not having a problem with that. How do you and I go there together?" That is how I do it.

How do I sign up for the advanced class? It is by application only, send an email to info@therecruiteru.com. We'll send you off an application. You and I will chat. Again, just for those who are intrigued, you will have access to all the same content, just a smaller, more intimate group with one to one access.

If you are in the monthly inner circle, $57 a month, and you want to sign up for solo recruiting coaching, do I have to pay for both? Yes, they are separate. The $57 a month, that is for the most part, I am interviewing other owners, other trainers, other experts in the industry, if you want to subscribe to that. It is not included with that but it is an entirely different thing. The monthly Q&A on the inner circle is emailed in questions that I answer. The coaching implementation, we are all there voice-wise on the call. If you like both, I think the $57 a month is a great investment to keep along with it because the content is entirely different.

How would you suggest that a client who has paid on a contingency retainer but are happy with me should pay me up front? That is a great question. I had full disclosure. When I started making this transition, I had some really good contingent clients. When they gave me an opening, I made the placement. I had no motivation to switch them to retainer. When I went to mostly retainer, I had some old school contingency clients where I was their trusted advisor.

My question to you would be, if you are filling 80%, 90% of the openings you are working with them on contingent, I would probably just stay contingent but I would let them know, "Geez Joe, you have been a great client. I am evolving my model to engaged-fee basis but you guys have been so good," and give them all the reasons why they have been so good. "As an FYI, I am not going to propose that with you guys." Here's what it does, it puts him on notice that if they take you for granted, you could propose a fee change, number one. Number two and more importantly, makes them feel special. I have always wanted that.

I had somebody I worked with that every year, their fee went up with me. They provided great value and I paid it, and it just rubbed me the wrong way. One of the things I always do with my clients and recruiting and I do with my coaching clients, when somebody comes in I have never raised their fees. I just think that shows respect, and that is why I would show them here. Show them respect by keeping their terms.

If however, you have made three placements with them and you have worked 20 with them, the way you get them engaged or retained to say, "I want to invest more seriously in your searches and you are not allowing me to do that simply because I know there are 47 people working on this so I can not go deep. I will continue to send you great talent that I have available but let's have a conversation."

"Let's have a conversation about what it could look like if I were the only guy to work on this and how that would increase the number of quality people you saw and how it would increase the number of people you are exposed to on the search. If you have a follow-up to that, John, I am happy to answer it. Again, if everything's really good there, I'd give it the same and I would just let them know it.

I was 3-for-3 and they love me. Okay, so you did. Then, just like what I said, just tell them you are evolving your model. You just have to put, "If I can use you as a reference, Mr. Client, you might be getting some people calling because as I am evolving my firm and my practice, I am going toward more of an engaged model. Now, you guys have been great. I am not going to do that with you. If they ask about financial terms, I would just ask you to keep that between us because you are getting a special deal and just talk about my ability to deliver for you."

By the way, when I began evolving from contingency retained jobs that is exactly how I did it. I called the people who loved me, as you just wrote about, and I told them they were getting a special deal. If they could just talk about my service delivery, not the financial terms because the financial terms were proprietary.

Do you have any references? I have got a ton. For this level of program, there's a bunch on my

LinkedIn page, Mike Gionta. You can read about their successes, send them an email. Just out of respect for their time, just as I would do with you, I do not want people calling. I am giving you two months to validate. If you have doubt that I am the guy, do not enroll. I try to be really sincere and honest with people, which is why I am giving you the two months out. Net, net, net, if you show up and you are passive and you listen, I am mildly entertaining but for $397 a month, there's probably better investments of your entertainment dollars. This is an investment in send me $300, have me send you $8,000 back because you will start doing the things that you have not been able to do on your own.

For those of you who are going at a high level, there's also the other solution that includes all this stuff. That is the Peak Performer Group I have talked about before. There's 20-something references up on my LinkedIn account. I have been doing this for eight years and they still invite me back every year. Hopefully, I am a little credible.

Do you put people in the group where you had equal billings or all level billings? If I had to draw an honest bubble curve, the $100,000 or $300,000 range is where you are going to find 80% of our members for Double Your Placements. People that do more than that generally want a little bit more of an intimate approach to go from $300,000 to $500,000 or $600,000 or something like that. Again, because of the higher-level group, I still give them access to all the same content, just a little bit more intimate side on the coaching.

What is the average fee you are seeing in today's market? 20, 25 or 30%? That is a good question and I do not want to answer it because I hear people getting quoted 20% a lot. It depends on the niche. Like medical device sales, that could be $12,000 flat, $10,000 flat. The average fee in placing certain types of nuclear engineers is $30,000 in engaged. Without context, I do not want to throw a number, and as strategy to stop quoting 20%, 25% or 30%. Start quoting numbers like 28.6%. Psychologically, it leaves you into an entirely different conversation. One of the things I can honestly say with my clients is wherever they have started at, we have evolved their fees up 4 to 8 percentage points off what they were by giving them a confidence of approaching the search in the right way.

I invite all of you who are intrigued with this, enroll in the program, look at those areas when we just did that exercise for that gap, as to what held you back. Those are the things we are really going to tackle. Those are the things you are bringing to the group call. Those are the things you are going to have access to me with as you begin to take some risk and get a little bit out of your comfort zone. You have got me there as a backup.

There are not a lot of $400 a month mentoring programs in the recruiting industry that do what I do. Actually, I am more expensive than the ones that are out there. I get better results. I have no problems sustaining membership in this program. People, once they joined, continue on with me in even higher level programs. In my heart of hearts, I charge $1,000 for this but I used to have a whole intake process of a month for this. Now, I let people self-select in. The people that execute stay. The people that do not execute leave.

I invite you again, **www.therecruiteru.com/solo**. I'd love to see you in the program. I can not wait to start working with you and having you see the same success as my other clients have seen. Working better relationships, getting retainers, having some more free time and a lot less chaos in your day and your week.

Thank you all for investing your time in reading this book and I look forward to working with you and growing your revenues. If you have any questions you can reach me at: **mike@therecruiteru.com**.

Testimonials

"I went through a period from late 2013 through the first half of 2014 where I had multiple deals blow up and despite growth in activity, placements would not come together. Then it all caught up in the second half of 2014, and my revenue grew 70%+ for 2014. His coaching was to follow the very specific activities (which he outlined in depth) we can control and that the placements would follow. I stuck with Mike's program and he was spot on. Net, net: I did almost double my revenues :-) I am very thankful I found Mike in the beginning of 2014 because I was still very new to the business, and might have given up. I'm so glad I didn't!"
Laurie DeSalvo, Founder, Career Movers, Inc.

"I first heard of Mike through some free coaching services he provided that were specifically tailored for small "niche" recruiting firms like Informative People Inc. From the very first call, Mike's been absolutely amazing and I was sorry I had not called him sooner! We've enrolled for the second year of The Recruiter U as we've already realized revenues that more than paid for DOUBLE the cost of Mike's program. He's a great guy, full of energy and practical, ethical advice. We'd recommend Mike's programs to anyone in the recruiting biz!"
Minda Hannenberg, Informative Recruiting, Las Vegas, NV

"2012 was a disastrous year for me as a recruiter. I started the year with high expectations but ended with dismal results. Largely out of desperation, at the end of 2012 I signed up for Mike's Coaching group as I hoped Mike might be able to get me back on track.

I have enjoyed being in the group and listening and talking to Mike 2X a month. This year is dramatically better than last, it looks like I will make the lofty goals I set for the when we started which I thought were largely a pipe dream.

I have gotten a great return on the time and money I invested and highly recommend Mike's Coaching Group. If you are struggling as a single shingle recruiter or have a small practice, I recommend you talk to Mike."
Rich Bond, Bond & Company, CT

"I joined Mike Gionta's Solo Coaching Group, because I wanted to learn the structures and ideas used by the best in this industry. Mike delivered that and more. I hit my annual goal in 7 months, making it my best year EVER... with 5 months left to go!

Mike, an expert in the field, led me and our group through the key concepts we needed to implement and provided feedback to keep us on track. I now have the same process and system that most seasoned recruiters use, which allows me to forecast my billings and removes the mystery in the business. My business is now engineered to deliver outstanding service while allowing more time for my family and travel. Mike's program generated these results!

I also can't say enough good things about Mike as a person. He is the definition of integrity: "adherence to moral and ethical principles; soundness of moral character; honesty," and makes working hard fun!!"
Beth Todd, Todd Legal, Chicago, I

"Our firm has received a huge return on investment from working with Mike Gionta and TheRecruiterU.com. I admit, we hesitated in making the investment in ourselves as we thought it was 'expensive'. I am glad we decided to move forward because one technique he taught us on one call has helped us realize an additional $49,000 in revenue alone! This is revenue we wouldn't have achieved based on how we used to approach the business, but now we are doing things the right way! Despite the economy, I am about to finish my best year ever thanks to my work with Mike!"
Mike Seminerio, Sales Consultants, Middlesex, NJ

Recruiter Resources

TheRecruiterU.com has numerous FREE resources available for both Solo/Independent Recruiters and for Owners looking to scale their business by adding great recruiters and creating systems for your business.

Visit **www.TheRecruiterU.com** to gain instant access to **FREE videos and audios** that will give you strategies and systems to get better clients, engagement fees, hiring million dollar recruiters, etc.

To get access to over $682 of Mike's training FREE go to www.TheRecruiterU.com/member for a trial membership in our Inner Circle Program. In this program Mike interviews highly successful recruiting experts each month on a variety of topics designed to give you insights to grow your business from the BEST OF THE BEST in the industry!!! Skeptical? That's why we offer you $682 in great training as an 'ethical bribe' to give us a no obligation trial in the monthly program. We even offer a full refund if you're not thrilled with the material!

See all the details for the RecruiterU's Inner Circle and enroll at **www.TheRecruiterU.com/member.**

Lastly, Mike has **advanced mentoring programs** (beyond the Double Your Placements Program) for both Solo/Independent Recruiters and for those recruiting firm owners that want office growth, hiring systems, and the ability to sell their firms for a premium.

If you are a Solo/Independent Recruiter that wants more revenue, better performing clients, higher fees, engagement fees, etc. with less work and more free time you may want to look into Mike's Peak Performer Program and is available by application only. For a no obligation assessment to see if or how we can help you please email **info@TheRecruiterU.com** for more information.

If you are a Recruiting Firm Owner who is SERIOUS in their growth and are seeking systems and strategies to hire future million dollar producers, if you are seeking how to have your business serve you versus you serving it, if you are seeking to lead a recruiting firm that runs without your physical presence .... you may be a strong candidate for our Platinum Coaching Program. For a no obligation assessment to see if or how Platinum can help you please email **info@TheRecruiterU.com** for more information.

Here's How to Double Your Revenue In the Next 121 Days Or Less...

You already know being a recruiter is one of the highest paying professions while providing incredible personal and professional flexibility. The confusing part is not knowing how stay out of overwhelm mode and make the switch from being a transactional vendor who gets no respect to a trusted advisor who is part of the inner circle on your clients team.

That is where we come in. We help people just like you put the strategies and systems in place to double your placements in just 121 days or less.

Step 1: We show you step by step how get clear on how your business serves you and how to engineer your time and your practice, to allow more life in your life.

Step 2: We stop the roller coaster revenue by leading you by the hand with the scripts and templates you will need to have **predictable income** month after month.

Step 3: We take you through the transformation when you go from **being a transactional vendor to a trusted advisor.**

Most recruiters struggle getting great clients (if they have any at all) because they sound like everyone else, thus are treated like everyone else.

Now you can double your placements by working smarter not harder. Learn how to differentiate yourself and get more consistent revenue WITHOUT the constant struggle!

If you'd like us to help, just send an email to: **info@DoubleYourPlacements.com** and we will take it from there.

Made in the USA
Middletown, DE
11 March 2015